MUCH ADO ABOUT NOTHING

www.**penguin**.co.uk

1   *No one much likes the title of this play, for which Shakespeare may not have been responsible (we don't know; no posters have survived). King Charles I spoke for all discriminating admirers when he crossed out 'Much Ado About Nothing' on the title page of his Folio copy and replaced it with 'Beatrice and Benedick'.*

The Incomplete Shakespeare

MUCH ADO ABOUT NOTHING[1]

JOHN CRACE

Annotated by JOHN SUTHERLAND

Doubleday

LONDON · TORONTO · SYDNEY · AUCKLAND · JOHANNESBURG

2   Shakespeare's theatre did not run to programmes, which is why characters use other characters' names so profusely in the early scenes. There may have been posters and playlists placarded at the entrance to the theatre.

DRAMATIS PERSONAE[2]

LEONATO	governor of Messina (appointed by Spain)
BEATRICE	niece of Leonato (resident in Leonato's household the past year)
HERO	daughter of Leonato
DON PEDRO	prince of Arragon
BENEDICK	gentleman of Padua, in the Court of Don Pedro
DON JOHN	Don Pedro's bastard brother, recently reconciled to him after a war
CLAUDIO	a count of Florence, in the court of Don Pedro
ANTONIO	Leonato's brother, an old man
CONRADE	associate of Don John
BORACHIO	associate of Don John
BALTHASAR	musician in the service of Don Pedro
MARGARET	gentlewoman in Leonato's household
URSULA	gentlewoman in Leonato's household
DOGBERRY	constable of Messina
VERGES, SEACOAL	watchmen, reporting to Dogberry
FRIAR FRANCIS	a priest
SEXTON	a cleric

3   *The play's setting is Messina, Sicily – but there is hardly a*
    more Spanish name and title than Don Pedro of Arragon. This
    might cause some perplexity for those not up to speed with
    pre-unification Italian history (i.e. most of us). Some context
    is helpful. The play is set at a time (present Shakespearean
    day, around 1598–99) when an unspecified battle has just
    been won. A band of victorious military men – officer-class
    blue-bloods, all (casualties have, happily, been minimal) –
    return for some rest and recuperation (and marriage) in the
    'house' (a palazzo) of the Sicilian Governor of Messina. At
    the time, Sicily was a Spanish imperial territory and the local
    government was delegated to trusted Sicilians. The noblemen,
    who are the principals in the play, are of both nations, Dons
    and Signors. Messina was a major cereal-exporting port –
    sailors knowledgeable about the place would be familiar
    around London's South Bank, where the theatres and many
    docks were located. It's worth remembering, too, that it's only
    just over ten years since England came within a whisker's
    breadth of being invaded by Spain in 1588 – horrible thought.
    Had they won, the Globe would have been performing plays
    by Lope de Vega and Calderón.

4   *A league was the distance a man could walk in an hour or*
    a horse cover in a quarter of an hour. Time was an easier
    measure of distance than 'miles' before accurate cartography
    (viz. a thousand steps).

5   *Who's the battle against? We never know. Leonato is not,*
    of course, thinking entirely about casualties, but ransom –
    always a painful experience for the gentlemanly class. Sicily,
    under Spanish domination, was subject to regular uprisings
    and rebellions by the indigenous population. Savagely put
    down, often. But let's not think of that.

ACT 1, SCENE 1

Messina, Leonato's house

LEONATO
I learn in this letter that Don Pedro of Arragon comes this night to Messina.[3]

MESSENGER
Indeed, my lord, he is but three leagues hence.[4]

LEONATO
How many gentlemen have you lost in this battle?[5]

MESSENGER
None of any note.

6   Claudio is 'Florentine' – from Florence. What he's doing in
    Sicily, fighting for what was essentially a foreign country, is
    never made clear. Money, booty, may have been the reason.

7   There's evidence that Shakespeare dashed off Much Ado in
    a hurry. The fact, for example, that most of it is in prose –
    quicker to get on the page than the iambic pentameter. This
    uncle of Claudio's, whom Shakespeare obviously thought could
    be useful in the plot, is never mentioned again. Leonato's wife
    Innogen also sinks without trace.

8   The battle between men is over; the merrier battle between
    the sexes has begun. Beatrice is concerned about Benedick
    (has he been killed, injured?) but doesn't want to show it. So
    she throws in a diversionary insult – a broad hint to the alert
    members of the audience. Why does she care? Is there an
    ulterior reason? Yes, indeed there is.

9   Shakespearean bawdy ahoy! There's a vein of civilised filth
    running through most of Shakespeare's comedies. The hero
    is, literally, 'well-dicked'. Only once in the play is he called
    'Benedict' – the term common in Christian blessing. 'Beatrice',
    incidentally, means 'the one who blesses'. The couple are, it's
    hinted, made for each other.

10 In old physiology, the stomach was associated with courage, as
    in the phrase 'no stomach for a fight'. We use the term 'guts' in
    the same way. 'Trencherman' is derogatory: Beatrice suggests
    that he is better at using his knife (trencher) for grub.

LEONATO

A victory is always so much sweeter when it's only the plebs that die. I hear that Claudio acquitted himself well.[6] His uncle will be pleased.[7]

BEATRICE

I pray you, sir, is Signor Humpty returned from the wars?[8]

MESSENGER

I'm not sure who you're talking about.

HERO

My cousin means Signor Benedick.[9]

MESSENGER

Oh yes, he's back.

BEATRICE

How is love's dream? Are all his loves still dreams? And how many hath he killed?

MESSENGER

He did good service, lady. He is a man stuffed with virtues.

BEATRICE

He is a valiant trencherman; he hath an excellent stomach.[10]

11 *Shakespeare wishes us to register the specifically Italian*
    setting. This is not his nowhere 'Illyria' or vague 'Bohemia'.
    The Latins – traditionally hot-blooded lovers – are as quick
    with a quip as a sword. They are passionate, not phlegmatic.
    The play opens with rapid-fire prose exchanges which alert
    the audience to a faster rhythm than in, say, Hamlet, *with*
    the sombre Scandinavian thud of Hamlet's decasyllabic
    soliloquies.

12 *In this play, 'wit'/'witty' generally means 'smart' – sometimes*
    downright smart-arsed. It is not 'wisdom'. Wit could also
    mean 'intelligence'. But here Beatrice's smartness alludes,
    by mention of the number five, to Aristotelian psychology.
    The Aristotelian five wits are: common sense, imagination,
    fantasy, judgement and memory. The more learned in the
    audience would apprehend that Beatrice knows her onions.
    She has been well educated.

13 *A joke about the dreaded syphilis – 'Neapolitan bone ache' –*
    associated with southern Italy. The disease was supposedly
    brought to Europe from the Americas by Columbus. Certain
    members of the audience would be nervously scratching their
    groins. There are innumerable pox jokes in Elizabethan and
    Jacobean comedy.

14 *The fact that he is a bastard – in both senses – is withheld*
    by Shakespeare until late in the play. The bard knew how to
    ration information, to keep the audience on its toes.

15 *Ironic. The leaders of a victorious battle would normally*
    receive a triumphant welcome back. Don Pedro's reception is
    strangely low-key. He notices. It irks him. He's easily irked.

MESSENGER

Are you calling him fat?

LEONATO

Take no notice. My niece always goes on like this
with Signor Benedick. It is a skirmish of wit
between them.[11]

BEATRICE

Faith that it were. In our last conflict, Benedick lost
four of his five wits.[12] By now, I fear he is but half a
wit. Pray tell me, who is his new best friend forever?
He hath a new one every month.

MESSENGER

He spends much time with Claudio.

BEATRICE

You mean he clings to him like a rash. Pray God,
Claudio has a decent supply of antibiotics.[13]

MESSENGER

Don Pedro is approaching.

> *Enter Don Pedro, Claudio, Benedick and
> Don John the bastard*[14]

DON PEDRO

You really shouldn't have gone to so much trouble . . .[15]

16   *The Sicilian governor kow-towing to his Spanish master.*
     Political tensions are already pulling the fabric of the action.

17   *I.e. Hero. The name ominously recalls an infamously suicidal*
     lover, memorialised in Marlowe's poem Hero and Leander,
     which was popular at the time.

18   *Cuckoldry is hinted at.*

LEONATO
It's my pleasure to near bankrupt myself
entertaining you.[16]

DON PEDRO
Is this your daughter?[17]

LEONATO
So my wife says . . .[18]

BENEDICK
And what say you?

BEATRICE
Oh God, look who it isn't. I was hoping you might
have got yourself killed.

BENEDICK
Not you again. I can't help it if all the ladies love me . . .

BEATRICE
All but me . . .

BENEDICK
Thank God for small mercies. For I have yet to meet a
woman who can touch my heart.

BEATRICE
You're just a commitment phobe.

19 *Given* Much Ado's *Italian and courtly setting, the literate*
    members of the audience would recall Baldassare Castiglione's
    The Book of the Courtier *(translated into English some*
    ten years before the play's first performance and, like Hero
    and Leander, *a bestseller).* Shakespeare clearly drew on
    Castiglione in the creation of Beatrice. Women, decreed
    Castiglione, should in the courtly world display sprezzatura.
    He invented the word – it is usually translated as 'quick
    vivacity'. Beatrice is sprezzatura *incarnate. In an English*
    setting, her smartness would brand her a shrew. And we know
    what happens to them, from The Taming of the Shrew. *They*
    end up kissing men's boots.

BENEDICK

Me? Me, the commitment phobe? You're the one with commitment issues.

BEATRICE

How do you work that one out? I was the one to whom you gave the 'I'm sorry, it's not you, it's me' crap last time.

BENEDICK

Jeez. I was only trying to be nice. It was you, not me, all along. I know what you're like. You came on all sweet but I could tell you didn't mean it.

BEATRICE

So you dumped me . . .

BENEDICK

That's a bit harsh . . .

BEATRICE

But fair . . .

BENEDICK

I merely got the dumping in first before you dumped me. In any case, there was a war coming up . . .

BEATRICE

And thank God for that. If not for your survival.[19]

20 He courteously omits to say 'half-brother'. Mixed blood, bad blood – for quite a long time past, we deduce.

21 Don John is the play's Machiavel (the philosopher Machiavelli argued that every prince should be a bastard if he wanted to keep a crown on his head). Being illegitimate renders John's marriage prospects nil. What does that mean? Revenge. Like that other blue-blood bastard, Edmund in King Lear, Don John will revenge himself on a society which, by the laws of legitimacy and primogeniture, has made him a non-person. If he weren't such a bastard we might feel some sympathy for him.

22 Claudio has already picked up the important fact that Leonato has no son – and, we deduce, is rich and old, with a wife who has disappeared in the twinkling of an eye. Kerching! Is that the rattle of gold ducats I hear? Claudio has left Florence as a 'soldier of fortune'. He's just seen fortune in a pretty dress with a nice hairstyle. We are already beginning to dislike him.

23 The text drops passing hints that Hero has brown hair (and a dark complexion, presumably), and is short. But Claudio, of course, is thinking of her other great attraction: the gold in her placket.

LEONATO
Enough. I invite all of you to stay with me for a month. (*To Don John*) And it's good to see you reconciled with your brother.[20]

DON JOHN
Thank you. I don't say a lot.[21]

LEONATO
I can see that.

Exeunt all but Benedick and Claudio

CLAUDIO
Did you note the daughter of Leonato?[22]

BENEDICK
I might have done.

CLAUDIO
And what did you think?

BENEDICK
Honestly? A B-minus at best. She's not my sort.

CLAUDIO
Well, I think she's hot.[23]

24 *They have not exchanged a word, nor spent more than a couple of minutes in each other's company. Hero has not heard Claudio's voice, we presume – that she hasn't will be essential if the trickery at the imminent ball is to be successful. We already understand Claudio for what he is. An opportunist. But not, at this stage, necessarily a villain.*

25 *What Leonato might feel about his only child being disposed of by strangers seems not to matter. Don Pedro is in charge.*

BENEDICK

You're mad. Even the gobby Beatrice is more of a looker than that minger Hero.

CLAUDIO

Well, I do love her and mean to make her my wife.[24]

BENEDICK

Please yourself. Ah look, Don Pedro is back.

Enter Don Pedro

DON PEDRO

What are you two up to?

BENEDICK

This idiot says he is in love and wants to get married to Hero.

DON PEDRO

She seems decent enough.[25]

CLAUDIO

'Tis true, I love her with all my heart.

BENEDICK

Oh spare us the saccharine. If I do ever tell you I am in love then I give you permission to kill me. Does no one but me want to remain a bachelor?

26 The Spaniard gives the Sicilian orders. Don Pedro is annoyed at the Paduan Benedick's uppitiness, and puts him in his place by treating him like a servant. This play is criss-crossed by subterranean tension of this imperial kind.

27 Horns and marriage go together like a horse and carriage. Italians were famous as lovers and, as husbands, for being obsessed with cuckoldry – the dreaded horns.

28 'Liege' was a leader to whom you had sworn an oath of allegiance, which took precedence over all other oaths – to spouse, governor, king. Sicily, as presented here, is notably lacking systems of order – courts, police, parliament – as we shall see when the forces of law and order make an entrance later.

29 The familiar 'thou' is significant from someone in authority. It suggests they like you. The sun is shining.

30 Claudio, falsely simulating love, flies high with an outburst of verse. It slows down the breakneck pace of the play – Shakespeare, it hardly needs saying, is a master of dramatic pace.

DON PEDRO

You say that now. But I do wager that within a month you'll be under some woman's thumb. Now run along and tell Leonato that I'll be joining him for dinner presently.[26]

BENEDICK

Carry on like this and you'll give me the horn.[27] I tell you, I'm not getting married.

DON PEDRO

Yeah, yeah. Yadda, yadda.

Exit Benedick

CLAUDIO

My liege, your highness now may do me good.[28]

DON PEDRO

Thou speak'st in verse; I guess thou art in love.
I'll gladly help, just tell me what thou wantst.[29]

CLAUDIO

Before the war, Hero I did quite like,
But now I find her hand doth come with cash
My heart doth soar, my loins are filled with love,
Or something close to delicate desires.[30]

31 *The man of power speaks. The fact that Don Pedro is in another grandee's house, taking it upon himself to dispose of another man's daughter and fortune, is irrelevant. He is the Don – just like Don Corleone, as played by Marlon Brando.*

32 *Masquerade. It's the prominent feature of Italian festivities (think of* Romeo and Juliet*). It represents the fact that everyone has an inner self, often very different from the outer self they choose to present to the world. Bear in mind that Hero and Claudio have not yet exchanged a word, as far as we know. If love it be, it must be love of the eye, not the heart.*

DON PEDRO

    Her father will not mind, of that I'm sure,
    I'll have a word and she will be your wife.[31]

CLAUDIO

    In truth, my lord, I am a little shy,
    I am not versed in ways of courtly love.
    Though I love her, what if she loves not me?

DON PEDRO

    Here's what I'll do: at the masked ball tonight
    I will assume thy part in some disguise
    And tell fair Hero I am Claudio.[32]
    And since she's bound to say that she loves thee,
    Then Bob's your uncle, she will be your bride.

33 Antonio is identified in early cast lists as an 'old man' – older than Leonato. What that means is that Leonato did not inherit the governorship, he was appointed. By the Spanish. Antonio may not like that. His younger brother lords it over him.

34 Servant? No, a spy. No court or large household was fully operational without its network of eavesdropping spies. In this case, it was what Don Pedro was up to politically that would have been of prime interest to the brothers. Leonato suspects there might be something for him in a union with the powerful, victorious Don Pedro (his daughter, of course, will do what he tells her to). He might, however, have second thoughts about a penniless adventurer like Claudio.

35 He doesn't trust Antonio, who may be playing a game himself.

ACT 1, SCENE 2

Leonato's house

Enter Leonato and his brother Antonio [33]

LEONATO

How's tricks, brother?

ANTONIO

You'll never guess what. One of my servants overheard Don Pedro telling Claudio how much he fancied your daughter and that he was planning to try it on with her at the dance tonight. [34]

LEONATO

Mmm. I wouldn't call that a wholly reliable source, but I'll go and tell Hero just in case. [35]

36 I.e. where there are no spies lurking about to overhear them.

37 His brother's 'niceness' is simply further public proof that
    he, Don Pedro, is in charge. In addition to being the play's
    Machiavel, John recalls another Elizabethan 'type', the
    Malcontent. Dangerous. As John Marston would anatomise
    four years later in his play of that name.

38 The name means 'drunkard' in Spanish. Presumably he lurches
    in, vino in hand.

ACT 1, SCENE 3

Outside Leonato's house [36]

Enter Don John the bastard and Conrade his companion

CONRADE
Why the long face?

DON JOHN
What's to be happy about?

CONRADE
You could at least pretend to be enjoying yourself.
Your brother is making a big effort to be nice to you.

DON JOHN
That's just making things worse. I can't stand having to
appear grateful when he's being so patronising. [37]

CONRADE
That's a bit harsh.

DON JOHN
Tough.

Enter Borachio [38]

39 *Don John has his own spy network. In the original play,
   Borachio claims he overheard this at a great dinner to fete
   the victory of Don Pedro. Antonio's servant claimed to have
   overheard about the ruse in the palazzo's orchard – a more
   private (and plausible) place.*

40 *Accompanied, presumably, by a drunkard's hiccup.*

BORACHIO

Top gossip. I was hiding behind the arras – as you do – when I overheard Don Pedro saying he would woo Hero on Claudio's behalf.[39]

DON JOHN

Suddenly I feel a bit more cheerful. I loathe Mr Perfect Claudio and here's my chance to wreck his chances. Here's to everyone getting food poisoning at dinner.

BORACHIO

Cheers.[40]

41 If 'the bastard' were truly reconciled with Don Pedro he
    would have been at his right hand at the banquet. That the
    invitation never came clearly rankled.

42 Beatrice is one of the longest female parts in Shakespeare,
    and certainly, given her high-octane personality and her
    volatile veering from tease to would-be murderess, one of
    the most demanding. In Shakespeare's time, it was played by
    a young boy. It was not until the Restoration that the part
    became one of the most challenging roles for a female actor
    in the whole Shakespearean canon. Up there with Cleopatra
    and Lady Macbeth. Stage history records the finest, most
    exploratory Beatrice as that of Ellen Terry in the 1880s. Terry
    'de-shrewed' Beatrice, creating a personality more deeply
    feminine and tender (as critics, all of them male, admiringly
    noted). Modern productions generally take a different tack.
    Beatrice is a rebel, a proto-feminist. She defies the 'chaste
    and silent' model of obedient maidenhood of her age. But by
    rebelling, Beatrice risks casting herself into three of the least
    attractive female roles in Elizabethan society – the shrew, the
    scold and the nag. And after her youthful years have passed,
    she will, if she holds true to her word, be something even
    worse: an old maid. Beatrice's main rebellion is that she talks
    too much and is grossly disrespectful of the 'superior' male
    sex. 'Lady Tongue' and 'Lady Disdain', Benedick calls her.

43 Beards feature in the play. As sweaty warriors coming home
    from battle, the men were still wearing them. But now they
    are perfumed suitors playing the great game of courtly love,
    with all its rituals, ceremonies and clean-shaven smoothness.
    Benedick does not conform. Will his martial face-fungus come
    off, or not?

ACT 2, SCENE 1

The great chamber of Leonato's house

Enter Leonato, Antonio, Hero, Beatrice,
Don John and Borachio

LEONATO
Was Count John at dinner?

ANTONIO
Not that I noticed.[41]

HERO
He's a miserable old sod.

BEATRICE
The ideal bloke is somewhere between Count John and
Signor Benedick. Someone who says neither too little
nor too much. Luckily, such a man does not exist.[42]

LEONATO
Why luckily?

BEATRICE
Because if he did, I might have to marry him.
Which would be a fate worse than death. You either
end up with a clean-shaven wimp or some bearded,
scratchy apeman.[43]

44 Scratchy like a cat, Leonato implies. It's in Beatrice's nature to be difficult.

45 He means dance. Which, being the senior person present, he 'leads' in both senses. The scene – which is notoriously hard to stage – is done as a masque, with disguised faces and a gentle accompaniment by the musician Balthasar, so as not to drown out the soft speech of the dancers. The dance, like the banquet, demonstrates harmony in Renaissance iconography.

46 Hero's little rebellion against her father. The play, and jokes about 'thatch', suggest she has seen his bald head and knows quite well who the old guy pretending to be the young guy is.

47 Needless to say, they both know who the other is. But, for the moment, they follow the rules of the game.

LEONATO
  'Tis thou who art scratchy.[44] I hope you're taking
  no notice of your cousin, Hero. She's just bitter and
  twisted. Now listen up: if the prince asks you to marry
  him, you know what to do.

BEATRICE
  You'll regret it, girl.

  Enter Don Pedro, Claudio and Benedick

DON PEDRO
  May I walk awhile with thee . . .[45]

HERO
  I hope your face is a bit less ugly than your mask.[46]

DON PEDRO
  Be nice. I'm trying to woo you.

  They move on in the dance

BEATRICE
  Will you not tell me who you are?

BENEDICK
  No. You'll have to guess.[47]

BEATRICE
  Well, thank God you're not Benedick.

BENEDICK
Who's he?

BEATRICE
Some idiot who's not half as funny as he thinks he is.
People laugh politely to his face, but behind his back
they laugh at him.

BENEDICK
I'll tell him that if I meet him.

BEATRICE
You do that.

BENEDICK
And thank God you're not Beatrice.

BEATRICE
Who's she?

BENEDICK
You wouldn't want to know. A total nightmare.

BEATRICE
I'll tell her that if I meet her.

BENEDICK
You do that.

They dance

48 *Borachio and John are out of the dance – plotting wallflowers. Who wants them?*

49 *Everyone is playing games. But since these dancers are all masked, how can the audience know who is who, and, more importantly, who is not who they claim they are? If the audience doesn't know, the plot falls very flat indeed.*

50 *By 'common', the bastard implies that she is of too low degree. Leonato (the point is frequently stressed) has no title, he is not in the aristocracy. John's deeper game is to egg Claudio on.*

51 *Ah, fickleness, thy name is Claudio. He has not even spoken to Hero yet, but in the course of a few hours he has 'loved and lost'. This play moves at the speed of light, so the audience doesn't have time to think. The question which lingers is why Claudio went along with the zany ruse of Don Pedro pretending to be him. A moment's reflection (one doesn't have time for more) suggests that Claudio knew Hero would see through the pretence and would understand that the man in charge, the Don, approved the marriage. But now Claudio realises his master may have stabbed him in the back.*

BORACHIO
　There's Claudio. I'd recognise him anywhere.[48]

DON JOHN
　Are you Benedick?

CLAUDIO
　I am he.[49]

DON JOHN
　Good. Since my brother likes you so much, perhaps
　you could have a word with him and tell him not to
　go chasing after Hero. She's far too common.[50]

CLAUDIO
　Are you sure he loves her?

DON JOHN
　On my honour.

Exeunt Don John and Borachio

CLAUDIO
　I'm sure the prince doth woo her for himself.
　Friendship for little counts o'er Hero's heart;
　'Tis each man for himself where love's concerned.
　No more my trust in princes will be placed,
　And as for Hero, she is dead to me.[51]

Enter Benedick

52 Beatrice has clearly hit home. Benedick cannot stop repeating
what she said, rubbing the bruises she has inflicted on his
ego. Clowns and court jesters were licensed to be rude – so
long as they were funny. But they had no social standing. And,
like the fool in Lear, if they overstepped the mark they would
be whipped. It's a shrewd thrust on Beatrice's part, who is
around 40–15 up at this point in the contest of wit. They laugh
at your jokes, but they don't respect you, she infers. And, of
course, she's largely right.

53 The characterisation of all the dramatis personae in this
play is paper thin, so as not to distract from the central,
spotlit, verbal interchanges between B&B. But Don Pedro, we
apprehend, is self-regarding. He fancies himself as a lover as
well as a warrior. A victor on both fields.

BENEDICK

Have you clocked that the prince has nabbed your Hero?

CLAUDIO

Thanks for the support, pal. But good luck to him.

BENEDICK

Any time.

CLAUDIO

I'm off.

Exit Claudio

BENEDICK

He'll get over it. At least he hasn't got to deal with Beatrice. She called me the court jester. What a bloody cheek. She's just bitter that I don't fancy her any more. I'll get my own back.[52]

Enter Don Pedro

DON PEDRO

Have you seen Claudio anywhere?

BENEDICK

He's just sloped off in a sulk after I told him that you had got off with Hero.

DON PEDRO

That's just not true. I was wooing her on his behalf. Pretty successfully, as it happens.[53]

54 *By this stage one is induced to wonder why Beatrice is so averse to Benedick. There are a number of possible reasons: 1. Benedick, as he boasts, is someone who uses women carnally for his own pleasure and self-esteem, as a 'gallant'. Loves 'em and leaves 'em. Shakespeare had already written* The Taming of the Shrew. *This is the taming of the womaniser. 2. Benedick may have tried it on previously with Beatrice, who opposes male hegemony. She is rude to him on behalf of her oppressed sex. It's not just Don John who's a bastard. All men are bastards. 3. Beatrice, oddly, has no father or appointed guardian to protect her. She is a woman alone. She is also, as we gather, penniless. 4. She may have lesbian tendencies. She loves Hero, and has shared a bed with her for a year (although this would not have been unusual at the time). It's a complex mix.*

55 *Will they, won't they? The verbal battle between B&B follows the line of the proverb* amantium irae amoris integratio est *('the quarrels of lovers are the renewal of love'). The paradox originates with Terence, a classical dramatist well known to Shakespeare.*

BENEDICK

If you say so.

DON PEDRO

God, you're hard work. No wonder Beatrice is always rubbishing you.[54]

BENEDICK

You think I'm hard work? That Beatrice would try the patience of a saint. Every time anyone tries to say anything nice to her she just shoves it back in their face. I'm telling you, she's got real commitment issues. Even if she were the prettiest babe in town – which, let's be clear on this, she definitely isn't – I wouldn't marry her.[55]

Enter Claudio, Beatrice, Leonato and Hero

DON PEDRO

Talk of the devil. Here she is.

BENEDICK

Get me out of here. I'd rather stick pins in my eyeballs than spend another moment with that woman.

DON PEDRO

Stop being such a drama queen.

BENEDICK

I just can't take another minute of her. I'm off.

56 One of the features of Much Ado *is the lack of any back-story,*
or any useful information about events before those we are
shown on stage. Information, for example, about the battle
a couple of weeks ago, about how well the principals know
each other, about the cause of the deep grudge Don John has
against his brother. Shakespeare withheld all this information
so the action could skim at high speed over what's going on
now, now, now.

57 *There is not a single soliloquy in* Much Ado, *which means*
we don't know, as we do in other Shakespeare plays, what
characters are thinking. The mask is never off the face. It
adds to the pace of the action, with its dizzying twists and
turns. This qualifies as Shakespeare's fastest play. It should be
performed at Usain Bolt speed.

Exit Benedick

DON PEDRO
You seem to have made quite an impression on
Signor Benedick.

BEATRICE
That's Benedick with the emphasis on dick. A while
ago we had this sort of thing going and then he did
a runner.[56]

DON PEDRO
So he dumped you?

BEATRICE
I wouldn't go that far. I don't get dumped. I'm the
dumper, not the dumpee.

DON PEDRO
I see. And what are you looking so glum about,
Claudio?

CLAUDIO
Nothing.[57]

DON PEDRO
Don't be such a baby. What more do you want? I've
done the wooing, Hero is sorted and her father's OK
with you both getting married.

58 Indeed. Claudio still has not, as far as we know, heard his
    lady-love's voice or seen her face close up. Shakespeare wrote
    his plays with the acting potential of his available cast in
    mind. It's a safe guess that the boy playing Hero did not have
    a lot going for him as a juvenile thespian. The crucial deal Don
    Pedro does with Hero and her father, clinching the lightning-
    fast and very dubious marriage contract, is done off-stage.

59 She is, as she says, 'sunburnt'. It is only in recent times that a
    tan has become desirable. The attractive female complexion
    in Shakespeare's day was pallor, indicating you did not work in
    the fields.

60 Don't call him Don Pedro, call him Don Fix-it.

61 Commentators have given this offer by Don Pedro much
    thought. Is it just his habitual droit de seigneur – he's top
    dog, he can have any woman he wants – or is he serious? It
    might make a useful political union. Or perhaps the poor
    old guy is lonely and he genuinely wants a partner. We
    assume he's not married. No children. If he doesn't get an
    heir, everything will go to the hated Don John. Shakespeare
    introduces these thoughts, then hurries on before the
    audience can give the suspicions serious consideration.

LEONATO

Indeed I am. Her cash is yours.

BEATRICE

You can speak, Hero.

CLAUDIO

I'd rather she didn't. Silence is sometimes golden.[58]

BEATRICE

Literally. Well, at least kiss him then. So that just leaves me on the shelf. Burning in the sun like a mat left out by the pool.[59]

DON PEDRO

I'm sure I can find you a husband.[60]

BEATRICE

I was being ironic.

DON PEDRO

But seriously. How about it? You and me?[61]

BEATRICE

That's very kind, but thanks but no thanks. You're not quite my type. I'm looking for someone with a GSOH.

LEONATO

I think you've said enough for one day. Run along.

62 Claudio plays the part of the trouser-busting warrior,
    desperate to sow his oats. But what, deep down, is his
    game? Shakespeare wants us to wonder. If Claudio were that
    desperate for 'relief' he could make a quick trip to one of
    Messina's houses of ill-repute. But he is still not certain that
    Don Pedro won't change his mind and scoop up Hero himself.
    And her ducats, of course.

63 What is his real plan? He's a commander – not a matchmaker,
    a balding Cupid. We deduce that in setting up these multiple
    marriages Don Pedro is creating alliances between the
    uneasy Italian and Spanish factions in Sicily. No more battles.
    Marriage among the high-born, in Shakespeare's day, was as
    likely to be political as romantic. It soldered things together.

Exit Beatrice

DON PEDRO
She'd make a good wife for Benedick. They're both
equally hard work.

LEONATO
They'd drive each other mad in minutes. Now,
Claudio, when do you want to get married?

CLAUDIO
Tomorrow. Love cannot wait.[62]

LEONATO
I think you'll find it can. Have a cold bath or
something. Another seven days won't kill you.

DON PEDRO
That should give us just enough time to fool Beatrice
and Benedick into falling in love with each other. It
won't be easy, but I've got a plan, so long as you all
help out.[63]

ALL
We will.

64 *The unmarriageable one. Who wants a bastard for a husband? Or, come to that, for a child. Who, one wonders, was Don John's mother? Probably a servant.*

ACT 2, SCENE 2

Leonato's house

Enter Don John and Borachio

DON JOHN
Well that went well, didn't it? So much for putting a
spanner in Claudio and Hero's works. They're only
going and getting married next week.

BORACHIO
'Tis true, I'm afraid.

DON JOHN
So that's me well and screwed. Everyone happy
but me.[64]

BORACHIO
Not necessarily . . .

DON JOHN
How so?

65 This is one of the nightmares for editors and commentators on Much Ado. *The simplest explanation is to assume 'Claudio' is a slip of the tongue – by Shakespeare or the dozy printer of the Quarto (printed, it's assumed, from Shakespeare's 'foul papers'), typesetting the first extant text of the play. If, as will appear, Claudio is watching the charade in the garden, how could he possibly be fooled into thinking that the pseudo-Hero is cheating on him by witnessing her canoodling with Borachio pretending to be* him? *Most performances cut the Claudio folderol and have Margaret ('Hero') misconduct herself with an unknown lover, showing herself to be a whore. Textual editors tie themselves in knots.*

66 This is a high-risk game the conspirators are playing for no clear reason. If found out, they quite likely will pay with their lives. Or exile, if they're lucky. *What, we must wonder, is the pay-off for the conspirators, assuming they succeed?*

67 Comedy is its label – but is it truly a 'comedic' play? Much Ado *has traditionally posed tonal problems for directors and actors trying to fix on the right mood and atmosphere. Should they go light or dark? The action verges at times on the very brink of tragedy. It could, at this point, quite easily go* Othello. *The modern preference is for dark.*

BORACHIO

It's like this. You know how I'm cosy with Margaret, Hero's maid? On the night before the wedding, I'll get Margaret to come to Hero's chamber window and shout down to me. She'll call me Claudio and I'll call her Hero . . .[65]

DON JOHN

And . . .

BORACHIO

And in the meantime, you will be standing nearby with Claudio and Don Pedro. As soon as they hear Margaret/Hero giving me the come-on, they'll reckon she's a bit of a slag and call off the wedding.[66]

DON JOHN

That is a truly crap plan.

BORACHIO

Trust me. We're in a comedy, where even the crappest plans work out.[67]

DON JOHN

OK, we'll give it a go.

68 Much Ado *is the Shakespearean play that investigates most thoroughly the codes of courtly love. It's worth looking at the cluster of words related to 'court': courtly, courteous, courtier, courtship. Courtly love, which originated in the castles and courts of medieval France, decreed that the woman should not be physically overpowered, bullied, or purchased, but courted into assent with graceful, silver-tongued wooing by a suitor who was, for the purpose, her slave. Hence the man's kneeling when making his proposal of marriage. Once married, he carries his bride over the threshold of his house: she is his property. What is significant about courtly love is that it allowed the wooed the power to say no. This is the moment in the play when Benedick will be transformed into a courtly lover.*

69 *He could, as do other spies in the play, hide in the arbour, behind a hedge. But Shakespeare wants to make him look ridiculous.*

ACT 2, SCENE 3

Leonato's orchard

Enter Benedick

BENEDICK

What a dreary old wuss Claudio is. Not so long ago
he was perfectly happy having a few beers with the
lads and then going on a killing spree the next day;
now he just whimpers about how much he is in love.[68]
I do hope that never happens to me. I'm not just
going to settle for any old woman. I want one who is
attractive, funny, clever and not too gobby. And such
a woman I've yet to meet. Oh God, here come the
prince and Mr Lover Boy. I'll hide in the tree.

Enter Don Pedro, Leonato, Claudio and Balthasar

DON PEDRO

See you where Benedick hath hid himself?

CLAUDIO

Indeed I do, he's dangling from the tree.[69]

DON PEDRO

Then let us moon like lovers oft will do.
Come, Balthasar, sing us a pretty tune.

70 Shakespeare did not adhere to the five-act, two-interval structure which posterity has imposed on his drama. One assumes this musical interlude is a moment of relaxation for the audience. Time out.

71 The song Balthasar actually sings is peculiarly appropriate:

> Sigh no more, ladies, sigh no more,
> Men were deceivers ever,
> One foot in sea, and one on shore,
> To one thing constant never.

72 The evening serenade is a crucial component in the courtly-love ritual. Ideally, as here, sung outside the lady's bed-chamber with a 'let me in, let me in' subtext.

73 Is Benedick talking, or merely thinking out loud? This is another of the staging nightmares posed by this play. He can scarcely bellow to the audience without being heard by the conspirators. We are meant, of course, to see him as a figure of ridicule, about to be taken down a peg or two.

BALTHASAR (*sings*)

Women are lovely, women are pretty,
That's all there is in this little ditty.[70]

BENEDICK

That's got to be the worst song I've ever heard.[71]

DON PEDRO

That's a top, top song. Come back tomorrow and sing
it outside Lady Hero's window.[72]

Exit Balthasar

DON PEDRO

Come hither, Leonato. What was that you were saying
about how much your niece Beatrice adores Signor
Benedick?

CLAUDIO

It's cool, he's listening. Carry on.

LEONATO

It's true. I wouldn't have believed it, but she worships
the ground he stands on.

BENEDICK

They're having a laugh, surely?[73]

74 *The thought flashes across one's mind that Leonato wants to get rid of the hussy, who's a thorn in his flesh – and not that close a relation anyway. Having a Beatrice in your house doesn't make things easier.*

75 *This would be a weak link were it not for the fact that Benedick is so vain he will believe anything that reflects well on himself. He is going to have to lose some of that narcissism.*

DON PEDRO

So she really does love him?

LEONATO

That's what she said.[74]

BENEDICK

It must be true if the old bloke says so.

DON PEDRO

Then how come she hasn't told Benedick this?

LEONATO

Because she's terrified that Benedick doesn't love her and will make fun of her. She doesn't take rejection well.[75]

CLAUDIO

It's true. My Hero tells me that Beatrice has started writing dozens of letters to Benedick telling him how she feels, but she never gets further than 'My dear Benedick', which she then crosses out and writes 'My darling Benedick'. Which is in its turn crossed out. She then writes 'Hi', before crumpling the paper into a ball.

DON PEDRO

Oh, she's a lovely girl, isn't she?

76 Don Pedro drops in another allusion to his princely droit de seigneur. *She doesn't have to love him – he could take her by right.*

77 Ominous. Shakespeare, from the first act onwards, drops a breadcrumb line of hints to warn the audience of dire things in prospect. *Laugh while ye may.*

78 The Elizabethans had various slang terms for this kind of trickery – if you fell for it, you were 'gulled' ('gullible', as we might say). It was described as 'coney catching' – snaring rabbits. Benedick is well and truly snared. This play is a veritable bag of tricks.

LEONATO

The best. And bright, too. In fact, the only thing
wrong with her is that she is in love with a man who
doesn't love her.

DON PEDRO

You're right, she's far too good for him. I wish she
loved me instead.[76]

CLAUDIO

Well she doesn't. And Benedick isn't that bad. He just
gets a bit stroppy sometimes.

DON PEDRO

Do you think we should tell Benedick how much she
loves him?

CLAUDIO

Definitely not. My Hero says Beatrice would rather
die . . .[77]

DON PEDRO

I'd say Benedick was hooked, wouldn't you? Now all
we've got to do is get Hero and her chums to play the
same trick on Beatrice and it's job done.[78] Let's eat.

Exeunt

79 *Not a single child to be seen in this play – Shakespeare adhered faithfully to W. C. Fields's rule: no animals, no children. Of the two – given Crab, in* The Two Gentlemen of Verona – *he probably preferred animals.*

80 *The suddenness and aimlessness with which Cupid's arrow can strike is a commonplace in Shakespearean comedy. But the Italian poet Petrarch (particularly in his sonnets to Laura) defined love as having connections with religious worship – an act not of lust but of reverence. One loved a woman (or a man) as one loved God. Love ennobled. A new Benedick is emerging here.*

BENEDICK

Well, knock me down with a feather. She really does love me, after all. And now I come to think of it, she's not so bad as all that. I will resolve to love her. Obviously it will be difficult because I am probably slightly out of her league, but I should at least make an effort. No one else will have her, and if everyone in the world refused to get married the place would soon be empty of people.[79]

Enter Beatrice

BEATRICE

I've been sent to fetch you for dinner.

BENEDICK

Fair lady, I thank you for your pains.

BEATRICE

It was nothing.

Exit Beatrice

BENEDICK

OMG, she does love me. The way she said, 'It was nothing,' after being made to walk down the corridor to get me. I think I, too, am in love.[80]

81   Hero has two high-born ladies in her entourage (both, like her, presumably looking for husbands). She, we deduce, is closer to 'Ursley' (as she calls her) than to Margaret. Who may resent that favouritism.

82   Margaret is one of the more interesting cameo parts in the play. The earliest cast lists describe her and Ursula as 'gentlewomen'. Not servants, but companions. This entourage identifies Hero as heiress to a sizeable estate (unlike Beatrice). Margaret bemoans her servitude. It is not Borachio's irresistible charm, but ambition to better herself that induces her to join a conspiracy which she must realise is a gross betrayal of Hero. Or perhaps she's just duped.

83   Eavesdropping dominates this play. In the Globe, which opened in 1599, the same year that Much Ado was, at a plausible guess, first performed there, there would have been stage-hands scurrying about between scenes with plants, signifying the garden, and (for Benedick's benefit) a tree big enough to hide in. Beatrice, incidentally, hides in a honeysuckle bush. It fits. Interior scenes would have the omnipresent 'arras' – a handsome draught-excluding wall-hanging, behind which an eavesdropper could hide himself.

ACT 3, SCENE 1

The orchard

Enter Hero, Margaret and Ursula [81]

HERO
    I find I have at last regained my voice,
    And can join in the fun with Beatrice.
    Good Margaret, run thee to the parlour
    And let my cousin know we talk of her.

MARGARET
    I'll make her come, I warrant you, presently.

Exit Margaret [82]

HERO
    Now, Ursula, when Beatrice doth come,
    Our talk must only be of Benedick,
    To make him sound the finest hunk alive.

Enter Beatrice

HERO
    Oh look, my cousin scampers to the hedge
    And doth kneel down to hear our conference. [83]

84 *As was said above, like Margaret, Ursula is no serving-woman, but a gentlewoman, capable of conducting conversation on equal terms with Hero.*

85 *There is so much deceit in this play that one cannot be sure how aware of the secret plot to wed B&B Hero currently is. She's not, as far as one can deduce, the smartest person in Leonato's house. Or even in her own bedroom, given what Margaret has in mind. One of the pleasures of this play is our curiosity, as spectators, about the game Shakespeare is playing with us. Canny old Will.*

86 *Ursula and Margaret have no reason to be fond of Beatrice, who is clearly closer to Hero (a bed-mate, indeed) than they are.*

87 *Even Hero is a bit frightened of Beatrice. What private conversations they have had, of a night together, we can only guess.*

88 *Beatrice, recall, is fortuneless – hence 'catch'. Sounds like 'cash'.*

89 *Why is Hero – belying her name – so pliable, so banal? In Marlowe's poem* Hero *and* Leander, *published only a few months earlier, the couple are lovers. Every night Leander swims across the Hellespont to woo Hero outside her bedroom window. She opens her window, finds him wet and naked, a night of love ensues. The similarities of the scene with Hero/Margaret at the high window and illicit love in prospect are obvious. Marlowe left his poem open-ended. In the Greek myth, Leander is drowned, swimming in a storm, and when she sees his corpse, Hero kills herself by throwing herself out of her tower window.*

URSULA

Pray tell me, Hero, how you heard the news
That Benedick loves Beatrice so true?[84]

HERO

It was the prince and my dear Claudio
Who begged me tell my coz of his amour,
But I did say 'twere best he were not told,
For Benny is too sensitive a soul
To bear disdainful mockery and scorn
That Beatrice would surely heap on him.[85]

URSULA

'Tis sure the lady can be quite abrupt
And that she doth find fault with everyone.[86]

HERO

But who doth dare to tell this to her face?
For she a temper hath, and no mistake.[87]
Though 'tis a shame we cannot make it known,
It feels not right that Ben should die alone.

URSULA

Oh do not do your cousin such a wrong,
E'en she must see the man is worth the catch.[88]

HERO

He is the only man of Italy,
Always excepted my dear Claudio.[89]

90 *Thinking, doubtless, of her own unfavourable marriage prospects.*

91 *In the play, using a familiar image for the subordination of an uppity woman to a man, Beatrice says that she will tame herself to Benedick's hand, like the trained hawk. The joke is, she can't.*

URSULA

Still, second best is really not so bad.[90]

HERO

Indeed it's not, and would that Beatrice
Could conquer pride and learn to be quite nice.
But she cannot and they must be apart.
So let's move on and choose my wedding dress.

Exeunt Hero and Ursula

BEATRICE

I can't believe my ears, can this be true,
That even my best friends think I'm a shrew?
Do they not see I have a tender side
That's hard to show, except in therapy?
Dear Benedick, love on, I will love thee.[91]

92 A man talking to men, the prince says he'll wait not just until the wedding, but until the marital deed is done and the blood-stained bedclothes are hung out of the newlyweds' bedroom window. Arragon, in central Spain, means a long journey of a thousand miles (or three hundred leagues in the play's preferred measurement). Don Pedro is going to report that his mission to Sicily has been successful. He has put down a rebellion and, by a judicious promotion of political weddings, cemented the Spanish–Italian settlement. He'll be expecting medals and promotion.

93 The famous lover's melancholy. The 'ailment' was reaching epidemic proportions in Elizabethan England. It was given a scientific treatment in Dr Timothy Bright's bestselling Treatise of Melancholy (1586). Shakespeare gave Bright's theory his fullest attention in Hamlet. According to Bright, two classic cases of the melancholic were the Forlorn Lover (Benedick) and the Political Malcontent (Don John). Women weren't allowed to be melancholics. It was exclusively a guy thing.

94 A grim little subtext here. Elizabethans neglected their gnashers. Elizabeth herself was missing so many that in later life it was, reportedly, difficult to understand what she was saying. Roll on, Colgate. The first toothbrushes didn't come into existence until the eighteenth century.

ACT 3, SCENE 2

Leonato's house

Enter Don Pedro, Claudio, Benedick and Leonato

DON PEDRO
I will stay until the marriage be consummated. Then
I'll go back to Arragon.[92]

CLAUDIO
I'll come with you, if you like.

DON PEDRO
That would go down like a cup of wet sick with
Hero. No, I'll take Benny boy instead. He's always
good company.

BENEDICK
I'm not at all well.

CLAUDIO
It looks to me like he's in love.[93]

BENEDICK
I've just got a bit of a toothache.[94]

DON PEDRO
Go to a dentist then.

95 He has lost his beard and is now a clean-shaven lover. His facial hair, Claudio says, is currently stuffing tennis balls. He has, of course, lost a big chunk of his manhood along with his whiskers. Benedick is now love's slave. Enfeebled, facially castrated.

BENEDICK
I haven't got one.

DON PEDRO
You're a bundle of laughs today. Cheer up, you're being a right downer.

CLAUDIO
He's definitely in love. He's had his rug cut, he's wearing make-up and he's wandering around with a guitar.[95]

BENEDICK
I'm just practising a new song . . .

CLAUDIO
Heaven knows I'm miserable now . . .

BENEDICK
I can't help it if I'm too deep for you. Leonato, you're a sensible man. Walk awhile with me, I've got something to ask you . . .

Exeunt Benedick and Leonato

DON PEDRO
Yes! He's in love . . .

CLAUDIO
And if Hero and Margaret have done their bit, then so is Beatrice.

Enter Don John

96 Don John is playing a dangerous game here. If he's discovered calumniating a pure woman, swords will flash and blood will run. His, perhaps. And, as for Don Pedro, the schemes he has been cunningly laying with so much ado will be foiled. And the rewards he expects in Spain will not come his way. That, of course, may be John's real motive – to scupper his brother.

97 Espionage and voyeurism are the key elements in this play. Its dark side is becoming ever more prominent. Leonato's house is Palazzo Paranoia. Suspicious eyes and ears everywhere.

98 Why drag down the whole of Leonato's house rather than just Hero the slut?

99 He feels guilty, and responsible, and vindictive as the matchmaker. Odd, however, that he doesn't ask Leonato a few questions.

DON JOHN
    A word in both your ears.

DON PEDRO
    What's up?

DON JOHN
    I know I don't have the best of reputations around
    here, but there's something you should know. The lady
    Claudio is getting married to is a bit of a slag.[96]

CLAUDIO
    My Hero?

DON JOHN
    Not just your Hero, every bloke's Hero.

DON PEDRO
    This cannot be so.

DON JOHN
    'Fraid so. Look, I know it's hard for you to take in, but
    if you just hang around outside her chamber window
    on the day before your wedding I can guarantee some
    bloke will turn up and she'll let him in for a bit of
    how's your father.[97]

CLAUDIO
    If this be so, I will humiliate her publicly at the altar.[98]

DON PEDRO
    So will I, mate, so will I.[99]

100 Dogberry, as we shall gather, is the 'master constable'. And very proud of it. The fact that he can't read or write is a bit of a handicap.

101 Verges and Seacoal are Elizabethan watchmen. On patrol every night in London outside the very theatre where Much Ado was first performed, watchmen were the predecessors of modern police. One of their functions was to act as talking time-pieces – 'Twelve o'clock of night, and all's well!' – also as security enforcers and peace-keepers. They were armed. They had rights of arrest and could refer suspects to magistrates – in this case, Leonato. Often individual householders would take up the unpaid watchman office, like a neighbourhood watch today. Verges calls Dogberry a 'neighbour', not 'fellow officer'. Watchmen were figures of fun and were generally despised.

102 Dogberryism = comically using the wrong word. Later called Malapropism (after Sheridan's play). From one or two slips in the first printed version it is clear that Dogberry was played by the company's great comic actor, Will Kempe. Imagine roaring in the aisles. 'Dogberry', incidentally, is a hedge weed.

ACT 3, SCENE 3

Near Leonato's house

Enter Dogberry,[100] *Verges and Seacoal*

DOGBERRY

Fancy meeting up with two other Brits in the middle
of Sicily! Are you good men and true?[101]

VERGES

Now you come to mention it, I suppose we are.

DOGBERRY

Good. Then you're all going to be plods for the night,
for you are truly desiring of that honour.

VERGES

You mean deserving.

DOGBERRY

That's what I said. Now who is the most
disqualified?[102]

SEACOAL

I can read and write, sir.

103 What's funny in the context of the play is how bad the
     watchmen are at watching. The company in Leonato's house
     are much better at it.

104 One of the legends about Shakespeare is that, as a lad in
     Stratford, he fell foul of the law for poaching – a night crime.
     He had a healthy disrespect for the watch.

105 The finest moments of the play pivot on verbal wit.
     Dogberry's witless clumsiness with verbiage shines,
     perversely, in the context of the virtuoso exchanges of B&B.
     The professional incompetence of London's night watch led
     to the unofficial profession of 'thief-taker' – bounty hunter.

DOGBERRY

Those aren't generally the sort of thing I'm looking for in a good copper. But since you appear to be a senseless fellow, then you can take the first watch.[103]

SEACOAL

So what's the craic?

DOGBERRY

The best advice I can give you is to do nothing. If you come across someone who is a bit pissed then tell them to deinebriate themselves. Intolerance always works a treat.

VERGES

I've always found you can't go wrong if you're having a snooze. What the eyes don't see, the police don't grieve over.[104]

DOGBERRY

'Tis true. It's never a good idea to get too close to crimsonels. If a thief approach thee, 'tis best to steal away.[105]

SEACOAL

So the best plan is just to sit on the bench for a bit and then go to bed.

106 *We should remember he's a very old man with very frail wits. Adds to the tension. But it's Seacoal who cracks the case.*

107 *Ducats, precursor of the euro, were current all over Europe. Italy would have had the scudo or florin. The watchmen are paid in English shillings – bobs for bobbies. The amount paid to Borachio is huge. In the original play it's hinted he has extorted it from Don John.*

DOGBERRY

Got it in two. But keep a vague eye on Signor Leonato's front porch as there's a wedding on tomorrow.

Exeunt Dogberry and Verges
Enter Borachio and Conrade

BORACHIO

I've had a hell of a night.

CONRADE

You sound absolutely hammered.

BORACHIO

That's only the half of it.

SEACOAL

This sounds promising. I must remember to pay attention.[106]

BORACHIO

I've just earned a thousand ducats from Don John.[107]

CONRADE

What for?

BORACHIO

It's complicated. First I had to dress up as a posh boy. Then I had to go and stand beneath Hero's window and call up to Margaret, 'I love you, Hero,' while

108 Why did Shakespeare not show this scene – as, for instance, he shows the balcony scene in Romeo and Juliet? One suspects it may have posed staging problems which the new Globe (if that was where the play was first performed) could not for the moment handle.

109 Borachio – perhaps because of his weakness for the bottle – is taking terrific risks by spilling the beans so promiscuously. He should grab his thousand ducats and scoot out of town as quickly as he can, while his head is still on his shoulders.

110 Another reference to eavesdropping, which the play hinges on at every crucial point. And the resolution (somewhat improbably, granted) is brought about by what? Eavesdropping. Neat.

Margaret shouted back, 'I love thee too.' The whole thing was completely nuts. You'd have thought Margaret would have wondered why I was calling her Hero and said, 'Oi, it's Margaret.'[108]

CONRADE

Maybe she was a bit out of it too.

BORACHIO

Maybe. Anyway, while all this was going on, Don John was in another corner of the orchard with Claudio and Don Pedro.[109]

CONRADE

And did they think Margaret was Hero?

BORACHIO

Yup. The pair of them went ape-shit, threatening to shame her in front of the whole church tomorrow. I don't feel good about any of this, I tell you. Especially the dressing-up bit.[110]

SEACOAL

I'm arresting you, though I'm not quite sure what for.

BORACHIO

OK, OK. We're coming quietly.

111   *The point is being made that Hero – the rich kid – has a sumptuous wardrobe and any number of garments that could serve as wedding dresses. That, too, may not have endeared her to Margaret, the snake in the grass.*

112   *The word 'heavy' indicates a premonitory feeling of gloom in Hero. Claudio has not sent her any love missive, one presumes. She feels something is wrong.*

113   *We gather, from remarks dropped by Borachio, that Margaret is a maid no more. Not virginal goods. And not. married.*

ACT 3, SCENE 4

Hero's dressing room

Enter Hero and Margaret

HERO
What do you think of this wedding dress?[111]

MARGARET
It's gorgeous. Suits you to a T.

HERO
It feels a little heavy round the shoulders; and I feel
oddly heavy too.[112]

MARGARET
It will feel a lot heavier when it's got Claudio on top
of it as well.

HERO
You should be ashamed of yourself, Meg.[113]

MARGARET
Don't be so prissy. A bit of bed action is half the fun
of getting married. Here's Beatrice, you ask her. She'll
tell you.

Enter Beatrice

114   *There are jokes in the text about 'a goodly thing, a maid*
       and stuffed, ho! ho!'. 'Stuffed' can also mean 'pregnant'. But,
       we deduce, Beatrice has been crying uncontrollably. She is
       losing Hero, her bed-mate over the last year. Make of that
       what you will.

115   *Again, Margaret is quick off the mark with vulgar*
       sexual badinage.

116   *Or possibly hay fever, from hiding in hedges. No, crying is*
       more likely.

HERO
　　How now, coz.

BEATRICE
　　How dow, sweet Hero.

HERO
　　What's the matter?

BEATRICE
　　I've got a cold. My dose is completely stuffed.[114]

MARGARET
　　And that's not the only bit that's looking stuffed.[115]

BEATRICE
　　Easy. It's me that normally makes the gags round here.

MARGARET
　　And yet thou has gone quiet.

BEATRICE
　　I've just got a sodding cold.[116]

MARGARET
　　Fair enough. Whatever you say. I'm only saying that
　　Signor Benedick has started wandering around like
　　a love-struck teenager and you're acting pretty much
　　the same.

HERO
　　Enough, you two. We've got a wedding to go to.

117   *The point is made in the text that not only is Verges better with the English language than Dogberry, but he is also older. However, he is also a subordinate in the crew and, as Dogberry likes to say, 'when two men ride a horse, one must ride behind'. Verges is constable pillion.*

118   *Why has Leonato not been let in on what has happened, setting him up for the most humiliating day of his life? The split between the Sicilians and the Spaniards is yawning. That will dwarf any marriage gone wrong.*

ACT 3, SCENE 5

The hall of Leonato's house

Enter Leonato, Dogberry and Verges

LEONATO
What do you two want?

DOGBERRY
Marry, sir, I would tell thee something in compliments.

VERGES
He means confidence. We want to tell you something
in confidence.[117]

LEONATO
Then do hurry up. My daughter's about to
get married.[118]

DOGBERRY
I would like to bestow all my tediousness on you.

LEONATO
You've made a good start. Though you could
do better.

119   *These are, of course, Borachio and Conrade. The local*
      watchmen have got a result. The real hero in the play is dear
      old Seacoal. Call him Sherlock. The name denotes free fuel
      washed up on the shoreline – from wrecks, mainly – and
      anyone's for the grabbing. It was highly valued.

VERGES

Comparisons are odorous. We are your loyal policemen subjects, sir, and we have been busy about your duty.

LEONATO

We're still not getting anywhere.

DOGBERRY

Very well. It's like this. We have comprehended two superstitious people and would have them put before you for trying.[119]

LEONATO

You've both been trying enough. I must be gone. Examine them yourselves.

Exit Leonato

DOGBERRY

We must leave no turn unstoned in the pursuit of jousting. Go fetch Francis Seacoal and let the excommunication begin.

120   If it is indeed a church, it would be the only church scene
      in Shakespeare. And a Catholic church, to boot. That would
      be tricky in Anglican England, in a licensed theatre under
      the Lord Chamberlain's strict censorship. It's unlikely
      Shakespeare took the risk of churching this scene in early
      performances of the play. The original setting was probably
      Leonato's parlour. In Victorian performances the spurious
      'church scene' was a lavish centrepiece of the play whose
      original essence was speed, not spectacle.

121   An example of wordplay with which Much Ado is replete. It
      is the Friar who will (as the congregants expect) 'marry' the
      couple – i.e. perform the ceremony.

122   The dismissive title, Much Ado About Nothing, is, we now
      realise, ironic. There is something of great and universal
      importance at the heart of this play. Beneath its fast-moving
      comic surface it anatomises the complex relationship
      between men and women and the social institution which
      traditionally exists to control that friction – marriage. And
      all is now in the balance.

ACT 4, SCENE 1

A church [120]

Enter Don Pedro, Don John, Leonato, Friar Francis,
Claudio, Benedick, Hero and Beatrice

FRIAR FRANCIS
Do you come hither to marry this lady?

CLAUDIO
No. [121]

FRIAR FRANCIS
I'll ignore that. Lady, do you come hither to be
married to this count?

HERO
I do. [122]

FRIAR FRANCIS
Is there any just cause or impediment why you two
should not be wed?

CLAUDIO
Can you think of any, Hero?

HERO
None, my lord.

123 Benedick, one assumes, turns to the audience, talking to them across the edge of the stage: there are a number of points in the play when the audience/player division is dissolved.

124 It's tantalising that we do not know exactly what Don Pedro and Claudio witnessed in the garden, under the window. Words, acts, false recollections of multiple improprieties? Did Margaret come down and 'lie' with Borachio? Or did he, more likely, go inside and upstairs? The big question, of course, is why, witnessing this act, the three soldiers standing yards away did not apprehend Borachio and beat him up? Why did they sneak silently away?

125 He knows the ways of soldiers, back from battle.

126 It is not a single unchastity, but multiple. She is 'stale' (a used woman), as the text calls her. Given the circumstances in which Hero lives – sleeping in the same bed as Beatrice, with two gentlewomen companions (spies, of course, reporting to Leonato), improbabilities mount.

LEONATO

Of course there isn't. Get on with it.

CLAUDIO

Well I've got one or two.

BENEDICK

This is beginning to get a bit lively.[123]

CLAUDIO

Dear Leonato, take her back again,
Give not this rotten orange to your friend.
For though herself she doth present as sweet
She knows the heat of a luxurious bed:
Her blush is guiltiness, not modesty.[124]

LEONATO

My lord, thou canst not both ways have thy cake,
If in her bed thou hast already lain
You can't expect her to a virgin be.[125]

CLAUDIO

Were that the case, I would not make a fuss,
But with each other we have been most chaste.
It is with other men she's played away,
And so I will not marry her this day.[126]

HERO

What's wrong with you? Why say you all these things?

127 Again, this is probably addressed to the audience, Benedick
acting not as participant but commentator. One of the
interesting dramaturgical fluidities in the play is that it does
not respect usual stage boundaries.

128 An allusion to the question in the Catechism, 'What is your
name?' – reminding us that this is ostensibly a religious
occasion. And as the more literate members of the audience
will appreciate, Hero in Marlowe's Hero and Leander
was unchastely not married to the lover who came to her
window.

129 I.e. on the wedding day itself. She is coming drippingly
unclean to the ceremony.

130 'Ruffian' indicates someone of the streets – a commoner.
Borachio must have laid it on thick in the garden. He really
ought to get out of town – unless he is waiting to squeeze
another thousand ducats out of Don John. Or stopping for
another drink.

DON PEDRO

> Upon my word, my friend doth tell the truth,
> I would not see him wed to such a tart.

BENEDICK

> It's not like me to state the obvious,
> But it doth look as if the wedding's off.[127]

CLAUDIO

> Let me but ask one question to your daughter.
> I beg you bid her answer honestly,
> For Hero must to Hero's name be true.[128]

LEONATO

> I give my word, she will not tell a lie.

CLAUDIO

> Hero alone can blot out Hero's virtue.
> What man was he, talked with you yesternight
> Out at your window betwixt twelve and one?[129]

HERO

> I talked with no man at that hour, my lord.

DON PEDRO

> Why then thou art no maiden. Leonato,
> With mine own eyes thy daughter I did see
> Talk with a ruffian upon that hour.[130]

131 'Exeunt' means a rather more serious exit in the case of
    Don John, who – if the actor playing him can get it across –
    realises what he's done and will make himself scarce as fast
    as he can. Thus, of course, making it almost certain that his
    plot will unravel and he will pay with his life.

132 Friar Francis will have taken her confession earlier that
    morning. And for many years before. He knows her even
    better than her biological father does.

DON JOHN
And so did I, for I was with my bruv.

CLAUDIO
O Hero! What a Hero hadst thou been
If all thy fair embraces meant for me
Had not misplacèd been on other men.
And so I weep and take my last farewell,
Though there be nothing fair and nothing well.

BEATRICE
How now, sweet coz, what doest thou down there?

DON JOHN
I think she must have fainted out of guilt.

Exeunt Don Pedro, Don John and Claudio[131]

BENEDICK
How doth the lady?

BEATRICE
                    She is dead, I think.
No, wait, she breathes and at me she doth look.

FRIAR FRANCIS
Yea, wherefore should she not?[132]

133   Leonato's paternal weakness is symptomatic here. One sees,
      at this point, why Shakespeare dropped Hero's mother,
      Innogen. She would surely have got in the way. And, of
      course, she would have defended her daughter from slander
      as her wimp of a husband fails to do, so worried is he what
      the prince, his master, will think of him.

134   Why not last night? Because she was weeping in the face of
      the imminent great changes to her life.

LEONATO

Wherefore? Why doth not every earthly thing
Cry shame on her? Herself she hath let down,
And worse than that, she hath let down her dad.
I'd rather she were dead than live with shame.
My Hero hath besmirched her kinsmen's name
And devalued our house's worldly goods.
Yet when I say My Hero, what I mean,
She is her mother's Hero and not mine,
There is no proof she comes from my bloodline.[133]

BENEDICK

Hang on a moment. For once I'm gob-smacked.

BEATRICE

Oh on my soul, my cousin is belied.

BENEDICK

Lady, were you her bedfellow last night?

BEATRICE

No, truly not, although until last night
I have this twelve-month been her bedfellow.[134]

BENEDICK

I did not have a clue you were so close
'Tis a turn-on, if for another time.

135 Leonato is terrified he is going to lose his governorship. Don Pedro will assume he knew his daughter was a loose woman. He is on very thin ice.

136 'Refuse me' here means 'disown me' – addressed principally to Leonato.

137 Benedick has kept his eyes open and has, as the text says, observed other 'villainies' perpetrated by Don John in the past. Don John's true colours are now on show. As his cowardice soon will be.

138 At last, some Italian spirit in the wimp. A bloodbath is in prospect.

LEONATO

We must accept the foulness of the truth.
Would the two princes and Claudio lie,
Who loved her more than any men alive?[135]

FRIAR FRANCIS

Can I just say that in my job I've met
Some women who are less than innocent.
But Hero doth not have the look of guilt,
We must to other explanations look.

HERO

If I have been untrue then let me die,
Refuse me, hate me, torture me to death.[136]

BENEDICK

Since the two princes are of noble mind,
It seems they must have been misled by John,
A bastard by nature as well as birth.[137]

LEONATO

I must confess I'm getting quite confused.
If Hero hath been false then she must die,
Yet if those that accuse her are at fault
Then I will seek my family's revenge.[138]

FRIAR FRANCIS

Now listen here, I've come up with a plan.
To buy us time, we'll say that Hero's dead.
For sure Claudio must feel some remorse

139 Shakespeare had his dutiful (Anglican) doubts about (Catholic) friars – viz. Friar Laurence, another grand schemer, in Romeo and Juliet. Slippery, two-tongued fellows all, the tonsured crew. But the Friar has judicial immunity. Not even the prince, Don Pedro, can punish a priest of the Church for telling him lies or fooling him.

140 And quickly, since it's hot weather and they are going to have to bury the 'dead' Hero soon in the family monument (vault). Her mother Innogen is presumably in there, after her brief appearance on stage.

141 Shakespeare is keen to get across that, underneath all her bravado, Beatrice is a sensitive woman.

On hearing his fiancée is no more.
And from his grief is sure to spring more love,
Such that her reputation is restored,
To let the marriage have a second chance.
And if this does not work and sorts not well
Then to a nunnery your daughter goes.[139]

BENEDICK

That sounds quite daft, but since I cannot think
Of something better, we will follow you.[140]

Exeunt Friar Francis, Leonato and Hero

BENEDICK

Well that was all a bit embarrassing. Have you
been crying all this time?

BEATRICE

Yes. And I'm going to carry on crying for a
while longer.[141]

BENEDICK

I'd rather you stopped. It's making me feel
uncomfortable.

BEATRICE

Tough.

BENEDICK

If it helps at all, I think your cousin has been wronged.

142   What is interesting is that in the crisis to come Beatrice
      shows herself to be twice the man that Benedick is – as, at a
      similar moment ('Kill Duncan!'), does Lady Macbeth. Already
      Benedick has dismissed any doubts he may have had about
      Hero's chastity. (Why, incidentally, has no one thought to
      interrogate Ursula and Margaret? They would have been
      sleeping in adjoining bedrooms.)

143   He has seen, as has the audience, the inner woman in
      Beatrice – weeping. But he makes the wrong response. Not
      love, but murder, is on her mind. She is, after all, an Italian
      woman. Daggers first, talk afterwards.

BEATRICE

If you were a proper man, you'd do something about it.[142]

BENEDICK

I am man enough to say that I love thee. Is that not strange?

BEATRICE

Not really. Now can we get back to the real business of sorting out Hero's mess.

BENEDICK

By my sword, Beatrice, thou lovest me.[143]

BEATRICE

Get over yourself.

BENEDICK

But you do love me, don't you?

BEATRICE

OK, OK, if you insist. I love you. Now how are you going to prove it?

BENEDICK

You tell me.

144 *Another zone of complexity in the play is its ingrained (or are they?) patriarchal assumptions. Men act; women can only react to what men have done, or will do. And, if they are very persuasive, what men will do for them. Beatrice cannot kill Claudio herself. Is Shakespeare affirming, questioning, or merely defining the boundaries of patriarchy?*

145 *By now Benedick will have come to a resolution. He could, of course, find a convenient time and place and stab Claudio in the back. Or get a couple of bravos to do it for him some dark night (as Macbeth murders Banquo). Or slip some poison (Claudius's preferred means of murder in* Hamlet*) into his tipple. But, being a man of honour, he must do it by challenging Claudio to a duel.*

BEATRICE

By killing Claudio, half-wit.

BENEDICK

I'm not sure I love you quite that much. Can't I just slap him about a bit?

BEATRICE

Don't be such an old pussy, you've got to kill him. Man up, I say. Hero has been wronged, slandered, she is undone. And Count Claudster is running around like some goody-two-shoes claiming that he has been hard done by. It's not right. If I were a bloke, I'd take him out myself.[144]

BENEDICK

Are you sure this is the only way?

BEATRICE

Are you deaf?

BENEDICK

All right, I'll do it. And don't forget to keep up the pretence that Hero is dead.[145]

146 Early stage notes identify the location as a prison, which would have been easier to set up on stage (some manacles and constables hanging about) than a courtroom. Modern productions do not have to observe such austerities.

147 The sexton is referred to earlier by Seacoal as a 'learned writer'; he's often described (following the first printed version of the play, the Quarto) in stage directions as a 'town clerk'. A sexton is usually someone working in a church, not a town hall.

ACT 4, SCENE 2

A courtroom in Messina [146]

Enter Dogberry, Verges, the Sexton, [147]
Conrade and Borachio

DOGBERRY
Is our whole dissembly appeared?

SEXTON
Which be the malefactors?

DOGBERRY
We are.

VERGES
That we are.

SEXTON
Where's the offenders?

DOGBERRY
Why didn't you say so? Here we have a knife called
Borachio. Say hello, Borachio.

BORACHIO
Hello.

DOGBERRY
And another knife, Conrade.

CONRADE
Gentleman Conrade to you.

SEXTON
Can we get a move on?

DOGBERRY
We are at your service.

SEXTON
It's supposed to be the gentleman of the watch who is their accuser.

DOGBERRY
That's a good pint.

VERGES
I'll just have a half. Calling Francis Seacoal.

Enter Francis Seacoal

SEACOAL
It happened like this. This bloke said Don John the prince's brother was a villain.

DOGBERRY
Calling a prince a villain is perjury.

VERGES
And you're getting away with murder.

SEXTON
What else did he say?

SEACOAL
That he had received one thousand ducats for accusing the Lady Hero wrongfully.

DOGBERRY
That's another charge of burglary.

VERGES
Don't be aggravating.

DOGBERRY
It's definitely not aggravated burglary.

SEACOAL
And then he said Count Claudio did mean to disgrace Hero before the whole assembly at the wedding.

SEXTON
Well, as Prince John has sloped out of town this morning and everything else has unfurled exactly as you have related, I have no choice but to send these two men for trial before Leonato.

148 It's odd that Borachio and Conrade do not realise what hot water they are in. It would be more plausible to have them hopelessly, slurringly drunk. Talking themselves into death row.

DOGBERRY

Come, let them be opinioned.

CONRADE

You are an ass, I say.[148]

DOGBERRY

Did you hear that? He called me an ass. I ask you.
I'm an upstarting gentleman. An ass! Write that down,
somebody, so it's not forgot.

149 'Reputation' – or, as the Spanish say (and wrote innumerable plays about), pundonor – *honour. What others think of you.*

150 *Leonato has no son to do battle for him. He has no younger brother. We suddenly see him for what he is – old. If the play gave us time, we might wonder (as we do in* King Lear) *how this old man happened to have such a young daughter. But there is no Mrs Leonato to answer that question, any more than there is a Mrs Lear.*

ACT 5, SCENE 1

Outside Leonato's house

Enter Leonato and his brother Antonio

ANTONIO
You are no fun when you bang on like this.

LEONATO
I will bang on unto my heart's content,
No man hath ever felt such grief as mine.
For I did love my daughter with my soul
And now her reputation is all lost.
What will the nosey neighbours think of me?[149]
Do not attempt to offer me comfort,
For thou can't know how 'tis to suffer so.

ANTONIO
Do not put all the blame upon thyself,
Make those that do offend you suffer too.

LEONATO
Good thinking, bruv, I like the sound of that;
The prince and Claudio deserve a slap.[150]

ANTONIO
Well now's your chance, for both this way do come.

151   *'Good day'. Shakespeare reminds us that no time has passed. Critics note that it makes sense to imagine this scene taking place not after the preceding scene, but simultaneously. Such simultaneity is not a device Shakespeare often uses, since it can confuse the audience.*

152   *There is only one older person Claudio respects, now the gloves are off. His patron, Don Pedro. One notes the scene is set outside Leonato's house. Claudio no longer owes him the courtesy of a guest. And he still half suspects that Leonato was part of the set-up, intending to sell him damaged goods.*

Enter Don Pedro and Claudio

DON PEDRO
Good den, good den.[151]

CLAUDIO
Good day to both of you.

LEONATO
There's nothing good about this day or you.

CLAUDIO
Talk to the hand, we are in a great rush.[152]

LEONATO
Thou werenst so quick to give me the brush-off
When thou didst hope to call me pa-in-law.

CLAUDIO
Don't take offence, we're meeting some old friends.

LEONATO
Too late for that, I'm mightily pissed off,
I'm spoiling for a fight; put up thy sword.

CLAUDIO
Calm down, old man, and put away thy sword,
You really should know better at your age.

153 Leonato does not yet have proof positive, but Shakespeare does not want the audience to leave the theatre thinking that he is a bad father. It would create a rather unpleasant aftertaste. So Leonato has to be swung round – rather improbably, given his earlier unfair diatribes against Hero – into the good-father role, prepared to surrender his life for his daughter's honour.

154 The only way the brothers can revenge themselves is by having Claudio kill one, or both, of them. He would then be for the high jump. Claudio has not the slightest intention of falling into that trap. He is not a hot-blooded fellow. Nor foolish.

155 Don Pedro is in too much of a hurry to get back to Spain to do what he should do, namely, look into the flagrantly suspicious circumstances of the garden scene (ask Margaret and Ursula some questions, for example). Even the bumbling watchmen are better detectives than he, the man in charge of it all, is. Shakespeare, we are gradually being induced to think, does not think much of the dago. Thank God God blew that wind that destroyed all those ships, and Queen Elizabeth didn't marry that Spanish king, Philip. A narrow escape for Albion.

LEONATO

    Don't patronise me, I will have revenge
    For the vile way my Hero thou hast wronged,
    And in the process also wrongèd me,
    Which is as bad, if not, in fact, much worse.
    So while she lies stone cold within her tomb
    I cannot let you pass without a fight.[153]

CLAUDIO

    Say what you like, I will not raise my sword,
    You are too old and would become road-kill.

ANTONIO

    Then since I am, despite my years, quite fit,
    Accept my challenge to a deadly fight,
    For I did love my niece and for her sake
    Would pierce the heart of any slanderer.[154]

LEONATO

    Steady, old boy, there really is no need,
    Though thy gesture hath not unnoticed gone.

DON PEDRO

    Enough of all this quarrelling, good sirs,
    We really are quite sorry Hero's dead,
    But what is done cannot now be undone,
    For naught can change that she was fairly loose.
    And since I am top dog around this town
    There shall be no more talk of duelling.[155]

156 *This scene is happening at the same moment that the deadly conspiracy is being uncovered. We are in a nick-of-time situation. If there is swordplay, things will be very serious indeed. And Benedick, we can see, is a man in a hurry.*

Exeunt Leonato and Antonio

DON PEDRO
　See, see, here comes the man we went to seek.

Enter Benedick

BENEDICK
　I've been looking for you too.

CLAUDIO
　You'll never believe it! Those two old codgers, Leonato
　and Antonio, challenged us to a duel. I mean, *us*.
　Think of the damage we'd have done them.

BENEDICK
　To be honest, I'm not really that bothered about how
　tough you think you are.[156]

CLAUDIO
　Lighten up. We've both had a tricky few days, what
　with finding my future her-indoors was having a bit
　on the side, and we could do with a few laughs. Tell
　us a few gags.

BENEDICK
　I'm really not in the mood for this.

DON PEDRO
　You a bit hungover or something?

157 *All will depend on which of them is the better swordsman. The bookmakers would probably lay odds in Claudio's favour. The point is made, early in the play, that he did such great things in the battle that he was immediately promoted to Don Pedro's right-hand man.*

158 *Don Pedro tries vainly to distract Benedick – who has hitherto been in his pocket. But Benedick now has another master/mistress.*

BENEDICK

Give it a rest.

CLAUDIO

Oooh, get you.

BENEDICK

Look, Claudio, a word in your shell-like. I'm deadly serious. You're a nasty piece of work. You've killed a sweet woman and you're going to pay for it. Name a time and place.[157]

CLAUDIO

Is this another of your gags?

DON PEDRO

Of course it is. Chill out, Benedick. Only the other day I was having a chat with Beatrice, and after the usual bit of banter about what a moron you are, she did inadvertently come round to saying that she didn't think you were as bad as all that.[158]

CLAUDIO

Which, coming from her, is as good an admission that she really fancies you as you're going to get.

DON PEDRO

So when's the wedding day, big boy?

159 How does Benedick know this? The bombshell in the courtroom has not yet become common knowledge. We must assume that after the (non) marriage he went to Don John to get the story of what happened in the garden. And discovered the villain had done a bunk. It's enough to justify his belief that Hero has been wronged.

BENEDICK

You're surprisingly chipper for two blokes who claim
to be distraught about Hero. Anyway, I've had enough
of the pair of you. I'm off. In the meantime, Prince, I
think you should know that your bastard brother has
skipped town.[159]

Exit Benedick

DON PEDRO

He sounded serious.

CLAUDIO

I'm sure he'll get over it.

Enter Dogberry, Verges, Conrade and Borachio

DON PEDRO

What are you doing with two of my brother's men?

DOGBERRY

Marry, sir. They have committed some fences, sir.
Fences so great they have taken gates, too.

DON PEDRO

What offences are they?

DOGBERRY

Secondly that they have committed slanders and sixthly
that they have belied a lady person.

160   *Borachio, we assume, is sobering up and realises that the only way he can escape the rope – or worse – is by making a clean breast of it. We never know if his desperate remedy works or not. Probably not.*

161   *Critics and producers of the play have, over the centuries, been in two minds as to whether Claudio is a shit or a simpleton. Modern, feminist-inflected performances go thumbs-down on him.*

BORACHIO

Let me just make things simple for you. I've done
wrong. I let your brother John persuade me to
woo Margaret who was standing by Hero's window
wearing her clothes, so that you would think that Hero
was having it off with someone else. I'm truly soz for
all the trouble I've caused.[160]

DON PEDRO

Who would have guessed?
This changeth everything.

CLAUDIO

Indeed it does, I'm sensing I've been had.

DON PEDRO

More than a bastard, also is John a cad.
I never really liked him, that's the truth.

CLAUDIO

And though it might have looked as if not so,
I never doubted Hero's innocence.[161]

Enter Leonato and Antonio

LEONATO

Which is the villain? Let me see his eyes.

BORACHIO

I cannot tell a lie, for it is me.

162   *Leonato is determined to get his pound of flesh. He may pay for it later, when Don Pedro makes his reports in Spain. Spaniards do not like to be publicly shamed. This is a play with many undercurrents as to ultimate outcomes which the audience will be pondering long after they have left the theatre.*

163   *He most of all, since he knew Don John best.*

164   *The fact that Antonio has a wife and daughter has been withheld. But Shakespeare has taken precautions against any suspicion that he is improvising desperately by having kept Antonio on the furthermost edge of the action.*

165   *A marriage of über-convenience, reminding us that in this world politics trumps everything.*

LEONATO

Thou aren't the only wrong'un in the room,
Here stand a pair of honourable men,
A third is fled that had a hand in it.
I thank you, princes, for my daughter's death.[162]

CLAUDIO

I cannot ask for aught but your revenge.
Gladly I do accept my punishment,
E'en though my fault were not really my fault.

DON PEDRO

The same for me, we were but gullible.[163]

LEONATO

No words can bring my daughter back to life,
But 'twould be recompense were you to go
To Hero's tomb and say a few nice words.
Then since you cannot be my son-in-law,
Perhaps you would consider marriage to
My brother's daughter. What say you? Nephew.[164]

CLAUDIO

I am not worthy of such grace, my lord,
Thy niece will do quite nicely, I am sure.[165]

LEONATO

That only leaves the problem of Margaret.

166 He is showing some decency. It will probably not save him or her. Hero's revenge on her gentlewoman companion will be extreme. She can expect to be flogged naked through the streets of Messina.

167 Modern productions find the pronunciation 'arse' irresistible. But the two words, although run together in American dialect, have distinctly different etymologies. Dogberry takes 'ass' to mean 'donkey'. The stupidest animal in the stable.

BORACHIO
I can assure you of her innocence.
Her only crime was being none too bright.[166]

DOGBERRY
Can I just remind everyone that the plaintiff called
me an ass?[167]

LEONATO
I'll take that into account.

Exit Dogberry

LEONATO
Until tomorrow morning, lords, farewell.

168 *The garden – created by a few props – denotes fruition. We are not told what season it is, but we can presume Keatsian 'mellow fruitfulness'.*

169 *This scene clearly presents timing problems. The notion of Benedick cosying up to the woman who so flagrantly betrayed Hero is beyond improbable. We have, again, to assume temporal concurrence. This and the previous scenes are happening at the same time. Ursula will rush on stage a little later to burst this pretty little bubble of comradeship between Benedick and the bad woman. We can hardly wait.*

ACT 5, SCENE 2

Leonato's garden [168]

Enter Benedick and Margaret

BENEDICK
Pray help me write a love song to Beatrice. [169]

MARGARET
Only if you write one about me. Why doth no man come over me?

BENEDICK
Be careful what you wish for.

MARGARET
You're not quite as funny as you think you are.

BENEDICK
Oh, sorry. Please will you go and get Beatrice.

MARGARET
Shouldn't be a problem. She's got legs.

Exit Margaret

170 *An act of female subservience, as in 'kiss me Kate' in* The
Taming of the Shrew. *But Beatrice is not tamed, and
probably – even after marriage (assuming Benedick survives to
marry her) – never will be. You want tame? Get yourself a dog.*

171 *One recalls Benedick's earlier comments about toothache.
Perhaps he does have halitosis and even his best friends
won't tell him.*

BENEDICK (*sings*)

> My Beatrice
> Is twice as nice.
> I know it's corny
> But I am horny.

Hmm, this song-writing business is trickier than
I thought. Now what word can I think of to rhyme
with luck?

Enter Beatrice

BENEDICK

Ah, there you are.

BEATRICE

So. Are you going to tell me what went down between
you and Claudio?

BENEDICK

A bit of trash talk. Now kiss me.[170]

BEATRICE

Foul words are but foul breath. And I do not kiss
foul breath.[171]

172 *The question he should have asked first. Shakespeare is using this rather odd scene to forecast what the marriage of B&B will be like. Constant witty bickering, with the hen pecking more skilfully than the cock.*

BENEDICK

OK, OK. I can't get out of the banter habit. Either Claudio accepts my challenge or I'll tell everyone he's a coward. Now, back to me. Which of my bad parts did you fall in love with first?

BEATRICE

There are so many, I wouldn't know where to start. But you tell me, which of my good parts you do suffer love for?

BENEDICK

I suffer because there are too few.

BEATRICE

I'm glad we've cleared that up then.

BENEDICK

Start as you mean to go on. And how's your cousin?[172]

BEATRICE

Extremely ill.

BENEDICK

And how do you?

BEATRICE

I'm extremely ill too.

BENEDICK

I guessed as much.

Enter Ursula

URSULA

Madam, you must come quickly to your uncle's. Lady Hero's been proved to be a saint, Claudio's been getting it in the neck and your uncle has been threatening to marry him off to some other cousin.

BEATRICE

Will you come with me to hear this news?

BENEDICK

I will live in thy heart, die in thy lap and be buried in thine eyes.

BEATRICE

Don't be such a soppy twat.

173 *The monument (i.e. grand family tomb) reminds us that we
     are in the world not of commoners, who make up the bulk
     of the audience, but the aristocracy. Aristocracy is expensive.
     Marriages among the nobility need to be carefully arranged
     to ensure the bloodline is preserved (no jiggery pokery in the
     garden), and, ideally, that sufficient wealth (in the form of
     money, land and property) is generated by the union.*

174 *A woman whom no one, particularly Claudio, has seen. She
     may be ugly. Since Antonio is ancient, she may be past the
     first, even the second flush of youth. What is being set up
     here is a test of Claudio's remorse for what he has done. A
     price must be paid. He cannot pay in money, he must pay by
     giving up his bachelor freedoms to a woman he has never
     met and probably can never love. He's up for it – if it turns
     out badly he can always escape back to Florence. Lots of
     beautiful women there.*

175 *There is no guarantee. He must wait for his unknown bride
     to die first. She may do it less conveniently than Hero is
     supposed to have done. And this – the point has been made
     over and over in the play – is a world where treachery is
     the rule. And if the garden scene proves anything, it is that
     Claudio is easily fooled.*

ACT 5, SCENE 3

Hero's Monument[173]

Enter Claudio and Don Pedro

CLAUDIO
Is this Hero's monument?

DON PEDRO
It looks like it. I'll just read the epitaph:
      She died a death of many cuts
      Slandered by some dopey klutz.

CLAUDIO (*sings*)
Here I give you my last song,
It will go on and on and on,
For I will sing till it is dawn,
Doing my best to look forlorn.

DON PEDRO
First light at last doth glimmer in the skies,
So you can stop and give us all a break.
'Tis time for us to go home and get changed,
Today thou will be wed to Hero's coz.[174]

CLAUDIO
Though Hero I did love, things could be worse,
For I get both a bride and all the cash.[175]

176 *Recall he heard her daily confession, and has done so for years.*

177 *She was fooled by Borachio, Leonato implies. It would have been easier if Shakespeare had given us the conversation in which she was persuaded to do the traitorous thing she did. The logical assumption, without that evidence, is that she was 100 per cent complicit. And will go to the wall.*

178 *Leonato is enjoying the sense that at last he, not Don Pedro, is in charge. He preens.*

ACT 5, SCENE 4

Leonato's house

Enter Leonato, Benedick, Margaret, Ursula,
Antonio, Friar Francis and Hero

FRIAR FRANCIS
Did I not tell you she was innocent?[176]

LEONATO
Yes, you were right. That's what you want to hear.
Though as it goes, the prince and Claudio
Were not as guilty as you had them be;
Just Margaret bears some fault for being dim.[177]

BENEDICK
Well I'm relieved at how it hath turned out.
I did not rate my chances in a duel.

LEONATO
Make thyselves scarce, dear ladies, for a while,
There is unfinished business to be done
With the noble prince and Claudio.[178]

Exeunt ladies

BENEDICK
Since you're here, maybe you'll help me out.

179 *What money does Benedick have? He may have been enriched by booty on the field of battle, ransom fees, or inherited wealth. Two cunning areas of total darkness in this play are the family backgrounds of the two principal characters, B&B. They may be heading towards love in a cottage.*

FRIAR FRANCIS
What do you want?

BENEDICK
Dear Leonato, doth thy niece love me?

LEONATO
I take it that thou meanest Beatrice
And not the one I give to Claudio.

BENEDICK
Indeed, it is of Beatrice I speak,
For I do love her as she doth love me,
And if it be thy will, I would be wed.

LEONATO
It's neither here nor there as she is broke,
But if it's what you want, I'll not complain.[179]

FRIAR FRANCIS
A double wedding means a double fee.
Here comes the prince and Claudio.

Enter Don Pedro and Claudio

LEONATO
Hast thou both come to honour thy promise
To wed my niece right now, though sight unseen?

180   *A bird in the hand. Claudio is relieved he has got off so lightly.*

181   *After the way he's behaved, we must assume this is not a*
      love match, but a political union designed to repair the
      damage done to national alliances in the awkward colonial
      set-up under which Sicily is controlled. Order must be
      restored. Marriage is one way of welding broken parts
      together. One can only imagine the post-marital rows.

CLAUDIO

I would not dream of failing on my word.
In fact, I would not mind another bird.[180]

DON PEDRO

Good morrow, Benedick, why the long face?

CLAUDIO

He must have fallen hard for Beatrice,
This mournfulness only befits the sick.

BENEDICK

Some signs of feeling would not go amiss,
Since thou art to be wed to second best.

Enter Hero, Beatrice, Margaret and Ursula, all masked

CLAUDIO

Let's get this over, I've got things to do.
Which is the lady I shall call my bride?

LEONATO

The same is she, and I do give you her.[181]

CLAUDIO

'Twould be a help were I to see her face.

LEONATO

No, you will have to wait until you're wed.

182 As Gertrude would put it, the lady doth protest too much. The double negative makes the point that we are not to take this statement at face value. But everyone, at this point in the play, is doing what they gotta do. What the restoration of order requires.

183 Again a question and answer in the Anglican Catechism. Religiosity is in the air.

CLAUDIO
Very well, my good lady, I'm your man,
I hope that thou art fit and love me too.

HERO
I loved you when I lived and when I died,
Never did I not love my Claudio.[182]

CLAUDIO
Art thou my Hero, whom I thought was dead?

HERO
The one and only, reborn heroine,
Who hath not yet reclaimed her voice to ask
You to say sorry for the wrong you've done.

CLAUDIO
Hold not thy breath, my sweetest, silent bride,
In Sicily the patriarchs do rule.
Let's to the chapel go and seal the deal.

BENEDICK
Before we go, which one is Beatrice?

BEATRICE
I answer to that name. What do you want?[183]

BENEDICK
Do you not love me?

184 *Wordplay, all the way to the altar.*

BEATRICE

        Tricky. Not so much.

BENEDICK

  I think thou tellest porkies, sweetest dove,
  For all my mates assure me that you do.

BEATRICE

  Do you not love me?

BENEDICK

        Tricky. Not so much.[184]

BEATRICE

  Thou also playeth false, my dopey man,
  For to my gentlewomen thou didst moon.

CLAUDIO

  See in this hand a sonnet what you wrote,
  Or something near it, to thy Beatrice.

HERO

  And I have here an ode by Beatrice
  In which she praises Benedick's big dick.

BENEDICK

  It seems we are busted, babe. There's nothing for it.
  We're going to have to get married.

185　*The Globe stage, insofar as we can picture it, did not have much machinery (and no lighting, of course, other than an open roof). But it had plenty of space. This conversation between B&B must be intimate; we should picture them separating themselves from the others, at the front of the stage, talking quietly, but loudly enough to be overheard by the audience.*

186　*What does the proverb say? Marry in haste, repent at leisure. One regrets that Shakespeare never did sequels for his comedies (as he did for his history plays). What kind of marriage is foreseeable for B&B? Certainly not a frictionless union. It's hard to imagine Beatrice taking the woman's vow of obedience seriously in the years to come. Or, come to that, Benedick not relapsing into his old womanising ways.*

BEATRICE

You're probably right, though I'm still not sure I couldn't do better . . .

BENEDICK

Oh do shut up. Just this once. And give us a kiss while you're about it.[185]

DON PEDRO

So how does it feel to be a married man, Benedick?

BENEDICK

Sooner or later, you're going to have to get over the fact that she turned you down, pal. But since you ask, I'm pretty damn happy about it. For the moment, at any rate. We'll have to see how it goes. But it's been a good enough first couple of minutes.[186]

CLAUDIO

Well I'm happy for you, because I'd have had to beat you up if you had turned her down.

BENEDICK

It was me who was going to beat you up, if you remember. Anyway, luckily enough everything turned out OK. Who would have guessed?

DON PEDRO

I'm not that happy.

187 *He must surely know there is no such woman. And where is Antonio in all this? Shakespeare has removed him. It may be a double part – one of the principals, when not on stage, may have made Antonio's few appearances. Critics have shown (most convincingly in examination of* A Midsummer Night's Dream*) how the Shakespearean troupe doubled and sometimes tripled up on roles.*

188 *This speediest of comedies ends in a hurry. What will happen to Borachio, Conrade, Margaret? How will Dogberry and his crew be rewarded for their detective work? Shakespeare lets such questions dangle in the audience's mind. It's all much ado about nothing.*

BENEDICK

Try to lighten up a bit. Why not get married? There's still that other niece of Leonato's whom Claudio was going to marry lying around somewhere.[187]

Enter messenger

MESSENGER

My lord, your brother John is ta'en in flight
And brought back here in chains to Messina.

BENEDICK

We'll worry about him later. Let's party on down tonight. We can always think of how best to torture the bastard tomorrow. Comedies. You've got to love 'em.[188]

John Crace is the *Guardian*'s parliamentary sketch writer and author of the 'Digested Read' columns, and he writes regularly for *Grazia*. He is the author of *I Never Promised You a Rose Garden: A Short Guide to Modern Politics, the Coalition and the General Election* and also *Baby Alarm: A Neurotic's Guide to Fatherhood*; *Vertigo: One Football Fan's Fear of Success*; *Harry's Games: Inside the Mind of Harry Redknapp*; *Brideshead Abbreviated: The Digested Read of the Twentieth Century* and *The Digested Twenty-first Century*.

John Sutherland is Lord Northcliffe Professor Emeritus of Modern English Literature at University College London and previously taught at the California Institute of Technology. He writes regularly for the *Guardian* and *The Times* and is the author of many books, including *Curiosities of Literature, Henry V, War Criminal?* (with Cedric Watts), biographies of Walter Scott, Stephen Spender and the Victorian elephant Jumbo, and *The Boy Who Loved Books*, a memoir.

TRANSWORLD PUBLISHERS
61–63 Uxbridge Road, London W5 5SA
www.transworldbooks.co.uk

Transworld is part of the Penguin Random House group of companies
whose addresses can be found at global.penguinrandomhouse.com

First published in Great Britain in 2016 by Doubleday
an imprint of Transworld Publishers

A CIP catalogue record for this book
is available from the British Library.

ISBN 9780857524270

Typeset in 11/13pt Berylium by Julia Lloyd Design
Printed and bound by Clays Ltd, Bungay, Suffolk.

Penguin Random House is committed to a sustainable
future for our business, our readers and our planet. This book
is made from Forest Stewardship Council® certified paper.

1 3 5 7 9 10 8 6 4 2